# What's in this book

This book belongs to

_____

# 去上学 Going to school

## 学习内容 Contents

### 沟通 Communication

说说交通工具
Talk about means of transport

说说乘坐方式
Talk about ways of transport

### 生词 New words

| | |
|---|---|
| ★ 路 | road |
| ★ 船 | boat, ship |
| ★ 坐 | to travel by |
| ★ 车 | vehicle |
| ★ 可以 | to be able to |
| ★ 汽车 | car |
| ★ 火车 | train |
| ★ 飞机 | aeroplane |
| ★ 问 | to ask |
| 骑 | to ride |
| 自行车 | bicycle |
| 地铁 | underground |

School Zone

## 句式 Sentence patterns

他们可以走路上学。
They can walk to school.

我们可以坐汽车上学。
We can take the car to school.

## 跨学科学习 Project

设计一款未来的交通工具
Design a means of transport for the future

## 文化 Cultures

交通工具的历史
The history of transport

# Get ready

**1** How do you go to school?

**2** How long does it take you to go to school?

**3** What do you think about the different ways of going to school in the pictures?

lù
路

zuò
坐

chē
车

chuán
船

kě yǐ
可以

很久以前，学生可以走路、坐船、坐马车上学。

qí
骑

zì xíng chē
自行车

qì chē
汽车

huǒ chē
火车

dì tiě
地铁

现在，他们可以骑自行车、坐汽车、坐火车、坐地铁。

他们走路上学很慢，他们坐汽车上学很快。

fēi jī
飞机

有人坐飞机上学吗？飞机比火车、
汽车、地铁快很多。

未来呢？大家坐飞船，还是坐飞天火车上学？

请问去星际小学要坐什么交通工具？

# Let's think

**1** Recall the means of transport in the story. Circle them.

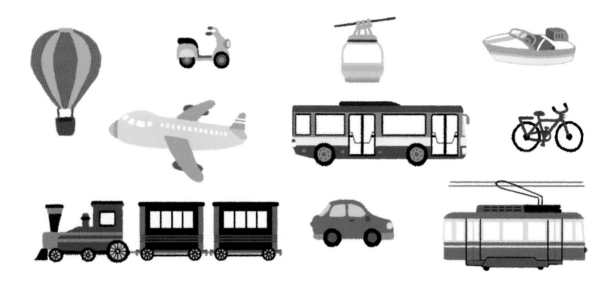

**2** Tick the transport that you have taken before. Talk about them with your friend.

# New words

**1** Learn the new words.

汽车

骑
自行车
路

坐 地铁
问

飞机    火车

可以

车    船

**2** Listen to your teacher and point to the correct words above.

# 听听说说 Listen and say

🎧 03 **1** Listen and circle the correct letters.

🎧 04 **2** Look at the pictures. Listen to the story a

**1** 今天男孩怎么上学?

   a    坐汽车

   b    坐地铁

   c    骑自行车

**2** 他们明天做什么?

   a    看电视

   b    玩游戏

   c    跳舞

**3** 男孩可以怎么去女孩家?

   a    坐火车

   b    坐汽车

   c    坐飞机

请问怎么去动物园?

你们可以坐汽车、坐地铁、走路去

坐地铁最快吗?

是的，坐地铁比坐汽车更快。

J.

动物园远吗？

不远，但是坐汽车比走路快。

我去坐地铁，你们呢？

太好了！我们也坐地铁。

**3** Write the letters. Role-play with your friends.

a 坐　b 走　c 可以　d 上学

请问你们怎么上学？

我喜欢 ___ 路上学，___ 多运动。

我坐船 ___，坐船很舒服。

我和很多朋友一起 ___ 汽车上学。

# Task

Do you know anyone living in another city? Talk about how you can visit them and draw the route.

我在香港，想去北京。我可以坐飞机，也可以坐火车去。但是不可以走路，也不可以骑自行车，因为去北京的路太长了！

# Game

Pick a word from each box and make a sentence. Say it to your friend. Is your sentence funny?

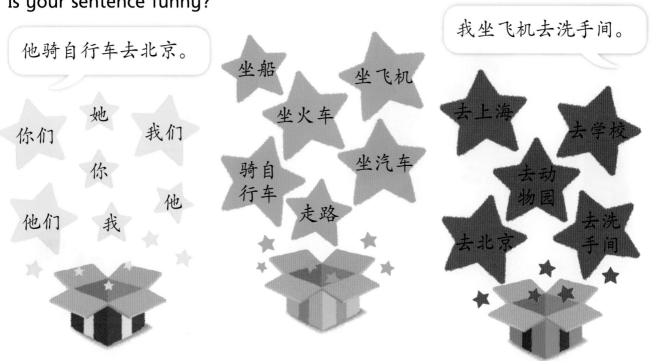

# Chant

05 Listen and say.

你坐马车，我骑马，
路上遇见问句好。
你坐汽车，我走路，
路上遇见说你好。
你坐飞机，
我坐小船，
他骑自行车，
打个招呼说再见。

生活用语 Daily expressions

可以，可以。

Okay.

怎么去?

How to get there?

# 写一写 Write

**1** Trace and write the characters.

、 丶 少 火

一 ナ 左 车

| 火 | 车 | 火 | 车 |
|---|---|---|---|
|  |  |  |  |

丶 冫 门 门 问 问

| 问 | 问 | 问 | 问 |
|---|---|---|---|
|  |  |  |  |

**2** Find out which character is missing. Write and say.

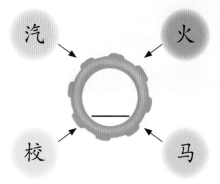

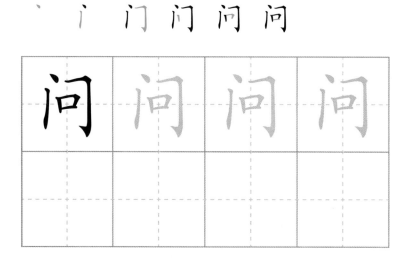

请＿＿我们可以
坐＿＿＿＿去北京
吗？

**3** Circle the wrong words in the paragraph. Write the correct ones on the lines.

火 山 莳 他 闷 时 夫 问 地

请间你知道这个城市吗？　1　_____

它在美国，是一个很冷的也　2　_____

方。我想坐水车去那里。因为　3　_____

坐车的吋间很长，我可以看到　4　_____

好看的雪田。　　　　　　　5　_____

## 拼音输入法 Pinyin input

The blue text is how we type the following paragraph, but there are some mistakes. Can you circle the mistakes and type the paragraph correctly?

When typing a paragraph in Chinese, leave two characters' space at the beginning. Do not forget the punctuation marks in each sentence of the paragraph.

Qunian bayue，women yiqi zuo feiji
去年八月，我们一起坐飞机
qu Beijing。gege zui xihuan tian'an'men, wo
去北京。哥哥最喜欢天安门，我
zui xihuan qu gongyuan zuò Chuan。mingnian wo haixian
最喜欢去公园坐船。明年我还想
qu zhongguo。
去中国。

## Cultures

Learn about the history of land and air transport. Talk about the pictures with your friend.

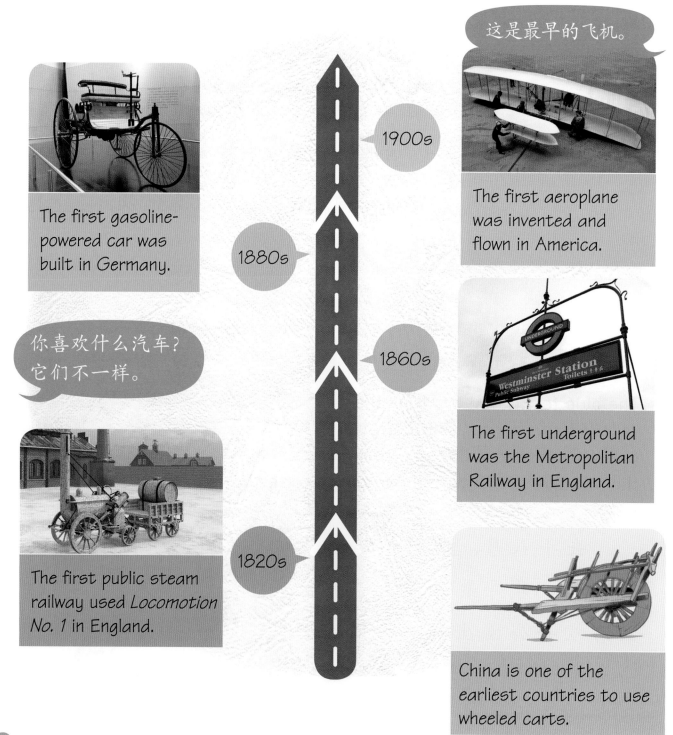

这是最早的飞机。

**1900s**

The first aeroplane was invented and flown in America.

**1880s**

The first gasoline-powered car was built in Germany.

你喜欢什么汽车？
它们不一样。

**1860s**

The first underground was the Metropolitan Railway in England.

**1820s**

The first public steam railway used *Locomotion No. 1* in England.

China is one of the earliest countries to use wheeled carts.

1  Match the means of transport to the correct categories. Which is your favourite?

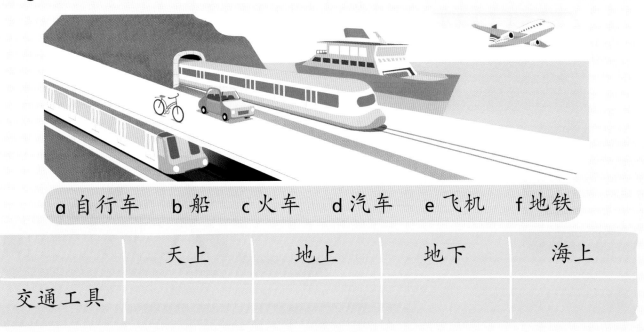

a 自行车    b 船    c 火车    d 汽车    e 飞机    f 地铁

| | 天上 | 地上 | 地下 | 海上 |
|---|---|---|---|---|
| 交通工具 | | | | |

2  Design a means of transport for the future. Talk about it with your friend.

这是……年的……
它可以……

它快吗？

它很快，比现在的……快很多。

你喜欢它吗？为什么？

我……因为……

# 温习 Checkpoint

**1** Help the children win free tickets. Write the letters and the characters. Can you get all the tickets?

> a 坐　　b 时间　　c 地方　　d 新　　e 比　　f 可以

### Air ticket

我们想坐飞机去中国。中国有很多城市，我们还＿＿＿坐火车去不同的＿＿＿。

### Ship ticket

今年，我想和我的家人＿＿＿船去英国。坐船＿＿＿坐飞机慢，但是很舒服。

### Train ticket

我最喜欢坐 ☐ ☐ 。

因为＿＿＿很长，我会有＿＿＿的朋友，我们可以一起玩。

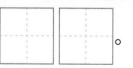

**2** Work with your friend. Colour the stars and the chillies.

| Words | 说 | 读 | 写 |
|---|---|---|---|
| 路 | ☆ | ☆ | 🌶 |
| 船 | ☆ | ☆ | 🌶 |
| 坐 | ☆ | ☆ | 🌶 |
| 车 | ☆ | ☆ | ☆ |
| 可以 | ☆ | ☆ | 🌶 |
| 汽车 | ☆ | ☆ | 🌶 |
| 火车 | ☆ | ☆ | ☆ |
| 飞机 | ☆ | ☆ | 🌶 |
| 问 | ☆ | ☆ | ☆ |
| 骑 | ☆ | 🌶 | 🌶 |

| Words and sentences | 说 | 读 | 写 |
|---|---|---|---|
| 自行车 | ☆ | 🌶 | 🌶 |
| 地铁 | ☆ | 🌶 | 🌶 |
| 他们可以走路上学。 | ☆ | ☆ | 🌶 |
| 我们可以坐汽车上学。 | ☆ | ☆ | 🌶 |

| | |
|---|---|
| Talk about means of transport | ☆ |
| Talk about ways of transport | ☆ |

**3** What does your teacher say?

My teacher says ...

# 分享 Sharing

## Words I remember

| | | |
|---|---|---|
| 路 | lù | road |
| 船 | chuán | boat, ship |
| 坐 | zuò | to travel by |
| 车 | chē | vehicle |
| 可以 | kě yǐ | to be able to |
| 汽车 | qì chē | car |
| 火车 | huǒ chē | train |
| 飞机 | fēi jī | aeroplane |
| 问 | wèn | to ask |
| 骑 | qí | to ride |
| 自行车 | zì xíng chē | bicycle |
| 地铁 | dì tiě | underground |

# Other words

| | | |
|---|---|---|
| 交通 | jiāo tōng | transport |
| 工具 | gōng jù | means |
| 久 | jiǔ | long time |
| 以前 | yǐ qián | ago |
| 未来 | wèi lái | future |
| 飞船 | fēi chuán | spaceship |
| 飞天 | fēi tiān | flying |
| 请问 | qǐng wèn | excuse me |
| 星际 | xīng jì | interplanetary |
| 回答 | huí dá | to answer |
| 更 | gèng | even more |

# OXFORD

**UNIVERSITY PRESS**

Oxford University Press is a department of the University of Oxford.
It furthers the University's objective of excellence in research, scholarship,
and education by publishing worldwide. Oxford is a registered trade mark of
Oxford University Press in the UK and in certain other countries

Published in Hong Kong by
Oxford University Press (China) Limited
39th Floor, One Kowloon, 1 Wang Yuen Street, Kowloon Bay,
Hong Kong

Illustrated by Anne Lee, Emily Chan and Wildman

Photographs for reproduction permitted by Dreamstime.com

China National Publications Import & Export (Group) Corporation is an authorized distributor of
Oxford Elementary Chinese.

Please contact content@cnpiec.com.cn or 86-10-65856782

ISBN: 978-0-19-082258-3

10 9 8 7 6 5 4 3 2